My United States

Maryland

VICKY FRANCHINO

Children's Press®
An Imprint of Scholastic Inc.

Content Consultant

James Wolfinger, PhD, Associate Dean and Professor
College of Education, DePaul University, Chicago, Illinois

Library of Congress Cataloging-in-Publication Data
Names: Franchino, Vicky, author.
Title: Maryland / by Vicky Franchino.
Description: New York, NY : Children's Press, an imprint of Scholastic Inc., 2018. | "A True Book." | Includes bibliographical
    references and index.
Identifiers: LCCN 2017000115 | ISBN 9780531252581 (library binding : alk. paper) | ISBN 9780531232880 (pbk. : alk. paper)
Subjects: LCSH: Maryland—Juvenile literature.
Classification: LCC F181.3 .F73 2018 | DDC 975.2—dc23
LC record available at https://lccn.loc.gov/2017000115

Front cover: Thomas Point Shoal Lighthouse

Back cover: A blue crab

Welcome to Maryland

Find the Truth!

Everything you are about to read is true *except* for one of the sentences on this page.

Which one is **TRUE**?

T or F   Maryland fought on the side of the South in the Civil War.

T or F   The Maryland colony was founded in 1632.

UNITED STATES

Maryland →

Maryland

5CW K37

www.maryland.gov

Find the answers in this book.

Contents

Map: This Is Maryland! **6**

1 Land and Wildlife

What is the terrain of Maryland
like and what lives there? **9**

2 Government

What are the different parts
of Maryland's government? **17**

THE **BIG** TRUTH!

Blue crab

What Represents Maryland?

Which designs, objects, plants,
and animals symbolize Maryland? **22**

Maryland's
state bird is the
Baltimore oriole.

The Preakness Stakes horse race

3 History

How did Maryland become
the state it is today? **25**

4 Culture

What do Marylanders do for work and fun?. **35**

Famous People **42**

Did You Know That **44**

Resources **46**

Important Words **47**

Index **48**

About the Author **48**

Maryland's state flower
is the black-eyed Susan.

This Is Maryland!

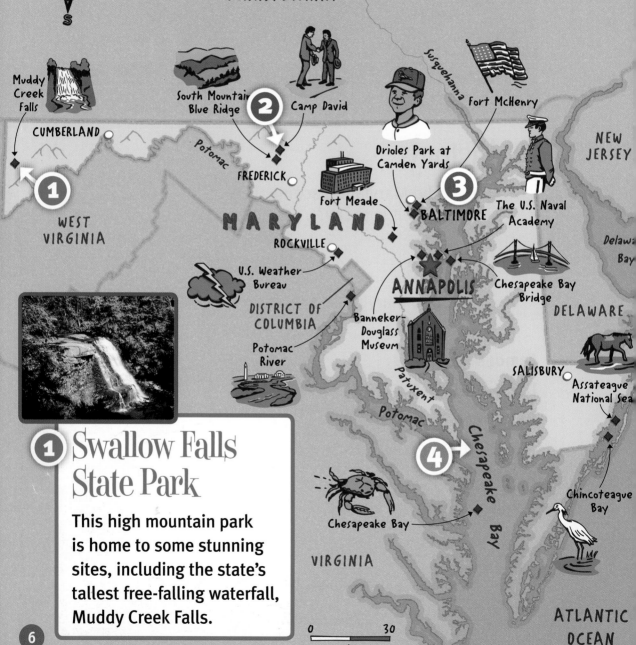

N W S E

PENNSYLVANIA

Muddy Creek Falls

CUMBERLAND

South Mountain Blue Ridge

2

Camp David

Potomac

FREDERICK

Fort Meade

Susquehanna

Fort McHenry

Orioles Park at Camden Yards

3

BALTIMORE

The U.S. Naval Academy

NEW JERSEY

1

WEST VIRGINIA

M A R Y L A N D

ROCKVILLE

U.S. Weather Bureau

DISTRICT OF COLUMBIA

Potomac River

Banneker-Douglass Museum

ANNAPOLIS

Chesapeake Bay Bridge

Delaware Bay

DELAWARE

SALISBURY

Assateague National Sea

Patuxent

Potomac

Chesapeake Bay

4

Chincoteague Bay

1 Swallow Falls State Park

Chesapeake Bay

VIRGINIA

ATLANTIC OCEAN

This high mountain park is home to some stunning sites, including the state's tallest free-falling waterfall, Muddy Creek Falls.

0   30
Miles

② Camp David

Camp David has been a favorite weekend getaway spot for many U.S. presidents. It was named after the grandson of President Dwight D. Eisenhower.

③ Baltimore

Maryland's largest city is home to many historic sites. It has been an important seaport since the 1600s.

④ Chesapeake Bay

The Chesapeake Bay is one of Maryland's most distinctive natural features. Visitors enjoy boating, fishing, and more.

Maryland's highest point and largest area of old-growth forest are both located in the Appalachians.

CHAPTER 1

Land and Wildlife

Maryland is sometimes called America in miniature. It's easy to see how it has earned this nickname. This small Middle Atlantic state is packed with a variety of landforms and wildlife. Within its borders are mountains, farms, cities, and beaches. There's a lot to see and do in Maryland!

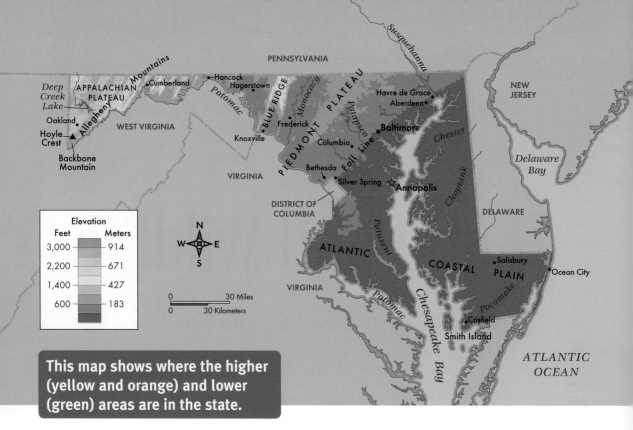

This map shows where the higher (yellow and orange) and lower (green) areas are in the state.

From the Ocean to the Mountains

Maryland has many different types of **terrain**. The state's southeastern tip touches the Atlantic Ocean. Farther inland, there are marshes, wetlands, and valleys. In the far west are the Appalachian, Allegheny, and Blue Ridge mountain ranges. The Appalachians are the oldest mountains in North America.

The Wild Horses of Assateague Island

Wild horses have been living on Assateague Island for hundreds of years. How did they get to this 37-mile (60 km) long island in the Atlantic Ocean? No one is sure. They could be the offspring of horses that were brought to work on the island. According to a popular legend, the horses escaped from a Spanish shipwreck. Remains from shipwrecks have been found in the area, so the legend could be true! The island is divided between Maryland and Virginia. It became a national park in 1965, and more than 300 horses live there today.

"Chesapeake" comes from the Native American word *chesepiooc*. It means "at the big river" or "great shellfish bay."

One Big Bay

A large body of water nearly cuts Maryland in half. This is the Chesapeake Bay. The Chesapeake is the largest estuary in North America. An estuary is a point where freshwater and salt water mix. Many plants and animals depend on the Chesapeake Bay.

Weather or Not!

When it comes to weather, Maryland has some of everything. In summer, thunderstorms, lightning, and floods are common. It is humid, and temperatures can reach above 90 degrees Fahrenheit (32 degrees Celsius). In winter, the eastern part of the state has mild temperatures. The western mountains can get ice storms and more than 100 inches (254 centimeters) of snow.

Kayaking is becoming increasingly popular in the Potomac River.

MAXIMUM TEMPERATURE	MINIMUM TEMPERATURE
109°F	-40°F

The loblolly pine is one of the most common trees in Maryland.

Growing Things

Many trees, flowers, and grasses can grow in Maryland's mild weather. In fact, the state is home to more than 3,000 plant **species**. Scientists know there were even more species in the past. They believe about 300 plants have disappeared in the state over the last 400 years because of pollution, development, and other changes to the planet.

Creatures of All Kinds

Maryland has numerous kinds of birds, mammals, reptiles, amphibians, and fish. White-tailed deer, foxes, beavers, and raccoons are found in much of the state. There are various types of frogs, lizards, and turtles. There are a number of ducks, herons, and songbirds. Almost 100 types of animals are **endangered** here. One of them is the Baltimore oriole, which is Maryland's state bird.

Maryland's oysters aren't just good to eat. They also filter water and help keep it clean.

The Maryland State House
is the oldest state capitol
in continuous use.

CHAPTER 2

Government

The city of Annapolis has served as Maryland's capital since 1694. This historic city was also the capital of the United States for a brief time in 1783 and 1784. Today, it is where Maryland's elected officials gather to make, **interpret**, and enforce state laws. These leaders also oversee a wide range of important services, such as the state's educational system and law enforcement.

The Three Branches

Maryland's state government has three branches: the executive, the legislative, and the judicial. Each branch has different powers. All three must work together to run the state. The founders of Maryland understood it was important to have checks and balances. This means none of the branches have too much power over the others.

MARYLAND'S STATE GOVERNMENT

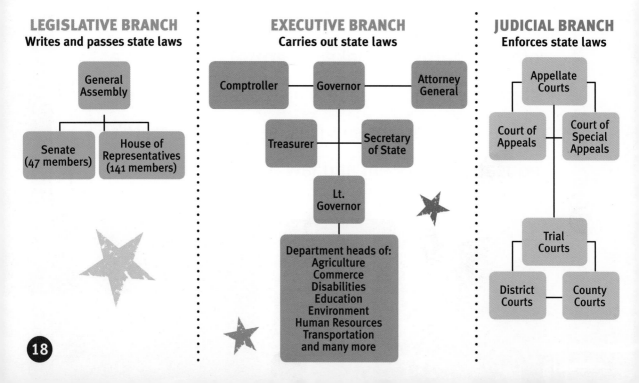

LEGISLATIVE BRANCH
Writes and passes state laws

- General Assembly
  - Senate (47 members)
  - House of Representatives (141 members)

EXECUTIVE BRANCH
Carries out state laws

- Comptroller — Governor — Attorney General
- Treasurer — Secretary of State
- Lt. Governor
- Department heads of:
  Agriculture
  Commerce
  Disabilities
  Education
  Environment
  Human Resources
  Transportation
  and many more

JUDICIAL BRANCH
Enforces state laws

- Appellate Courts
  - Court of Appeals
  - Court of Special Appeals
- Trial Courts
  - District Courts
  - County Courts

At the NASA Goddard Space Flight Center in Greenbelt, a worker makes adjustments to a piece of the Hubble Space Telescope.

Close to the Capital

Because Maryland is located so close to the U.S. capital, Washington, D.C., it is home to many federal government offices. The National Security Agency and the U.S. Census Bureau are both headquartered in Maryland. The U.S. military and the National Aeronautics and Space Administration (NASA) also have facilities there.

Maryland's National Role

Each state sends elected officials to represent it in the U.S. Congress. Like every state, Maryland has two senators. The U.S. House of Representatives relies on a state's population to determine its numbers. Maryland has eight representatives in the House.

Every four years, states vote on the next U.S. president. Each state is granted a number of electoral votes based on its members in Congress. With two senators and eight representatives, Maryland has 10 electoral votes.

2 senators and 8 representatives

10 electoral votes

With 10 electoral votes, Maryland's voice in presidential elections is about average compared to other states.

Representing Maryland

Elected officials in Maryland represent a population with a range of interests, lifestyles, and backgrounds.

Ethnicity (2015 estimates)

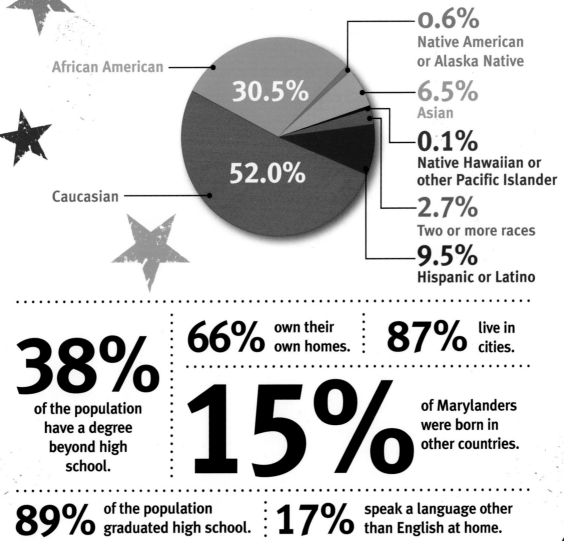

African American — 30.5%

Caucasian — 52.0%

0.6% Native American or Alaska Native

6.5% Asian

0.1% Native Hawaiian or other Pacific Islander

2.7% Two or more races

9.5% Hispanic or Latino

38% of the population have a degree beyond high school.

66% own their own homes.

87% live in cities.

15% of Marylanders were born in other countries.

89% of the population graduated high school.

17% speak a language other than English at home.

What Represents Maryland?

States choose specific animals, plants, and objects to represent the values and characteristics of the land and its people. Find out why these symbols were chosen to represent Maryland or discover surprising curiosities about them.

Seal

The shield on Maryland's seal shows two coats of arms, or family symbols, of the Calvert family. This family helped start the Maryland **colony**. A farmer on the left and a fisher on the right hold the shield.

Flag

Maryland's flag matches the shield on the state seal. The two designs are Calvert family coats of arms.

Black-Eyed Susan

STATE FLOWER

This sunflower, with colors matching the state flag, has long been popular in Maryland and is even the subject of a song.

Blue Crab

STATE CRUSTACEAN

The blue crab's scientific name, *Callinectes sapidus*, means, "beautiful swimmer that is savory."

Smith Island Cake

STATE DESSERT

This 10-layer cake comes from Smith Island, a difficult-to-reach island in the Chesapeake Bay with a culture all its own.

Jousting

STATE SPORT

Maryland has held jousting tournaments since colonial times.

Baltimore Oriole

STATE BIRD

With similar coloring to the state flag, this bird provides the name for the state's professional baseball team.

Patuxent River Stone

STATE GEM

The Patuxent River stone is a type of quartz that is found only in Maryland.

Native Americans taught the first English colonists in Maryland how to plant local crops.

CHAPTER 3

History

Maryland has a long and interesting history. Native people first settled the land that became Maryland about 12,000 years ago. Later it was a British colony and one of the original 13 states. Maryland has played an important role in the country for more than 200 years. Today, it is home to some of the world's most famous universities and companies.

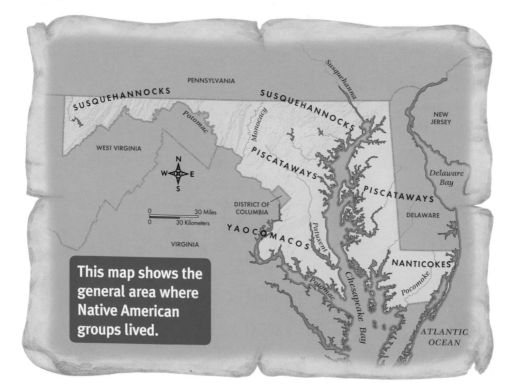

This map shows the general area where Native American groups lived.

First People

Archaeologists believe people have lived in Maryland for more than 12,000 years. How do they know? They study clues from stone tools and burial sites. By about 1000 CE, thousands of Native Americans lived in Maryland. They hunted and fished for food. They also grew crops such as beans, squash, and corn.

Native Americans

Around 1300, a Native American group called the Algonquins began to move into Maryland. They gathered oysters from the sea. They hollowed out trees and made canoes. They turned wood into bows and arrows. Sometimes Algonquins traded what they grew or made with other native people. They lived in dome-shaped houses called wigwams. These homes had wooden frames that were covered with animal skins and bark to keep out the cold.

Many different native groups used wigwams.

The Europeans Arrive

In the late 1400s and early 1500s, European explorers traveled across the ocean. France, Spain, and England all wanted the land near the Chesapeake Bay, but the English built the area's first settlement. In 1632, King Charles I gave land to Cecilius Calvert, Lord Baltimore, to create the colony of Maryland. These were hard times for the Native Americans. Many died of diseases brought by the Europeans. Others were forced to leave their land.

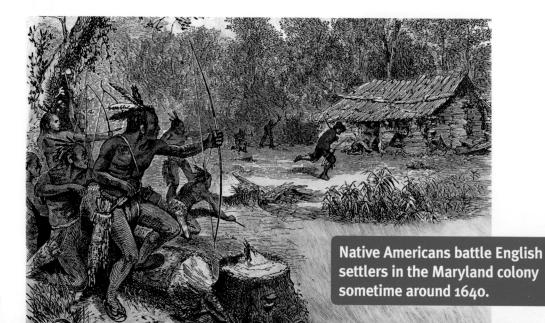

Native Americans battle English settlers in the Maryland colony sometime around 1640.

People from across the 13 colonies fought to establish a new, independent country.

A New Nation

Maryland was one of the original 13 British colonies. Colonists were citizens of Great Britain, but they did not have a say in the British government. The government demanded that the colonists pay high **taxes**, causing many colonists to become unhappy with British rule. During the Revolutionary War (1775–1783), the colonies fought to become independent from Great Britain. In 1788, Maryland became the seventh state of the new United States.

The Question of Slavery

Many people in Maryland were farmers. They wanted workers to run their farms. Some used slaves from Africa. During the Civil War (1861–1865), Maryland had to decide if it would side with the North or South. The North wanted to end slavery, and the South did not. Maryland remained with the North, although many people in the state did not agree.

Timeline of Maryland Events

April 28, 1788
Maryland becomes the seventh state.

1791
Maryland donates land for the new U.S. capital, Washington D.C.

1632	1788	1791	1862

1632
King Charles I of Great Britain gives a charter to Cecilius Calvert to create the Maryland colony.

1862
The Battle of Antietam, the bloodiest battle of the Civil War, takes place in Maryland.

Maryland was also the site of one of the Civil War's biggest battles. On September 17, 1862, Northern and Southern forces clashed near Antietam Creek in the town of Sharpsburg. The Battle of Antietam was the first battle of the war to take place in the North. More than 22,000 people were injured or killed that day, making it the bloodiest battle ever to take place on U.S. soil.

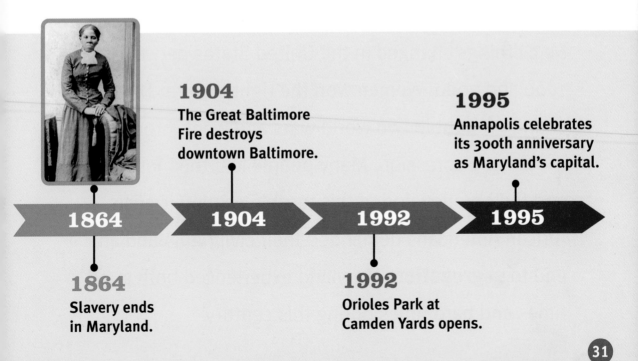

1904
The Great Baltimore Fire destroys downtown Baltimore.

1995
Annapolis celebrates its 300th anniversary as Maryland's capital.

1864 | **1904** | **1992** | **1995**

1864
Slavery ends in Maryland.

1992
Orioles Park at Camden Yards opens.

During World War II, many women went to work at the Bethlehem-Fairfield Shipyards in Baltimore.

Changing Times

Many things changed in the United States between 1900 and 2000. Women won the right to vote. The country fought in two world wars and went through the Great Depression. Many people lost their jobs and their money during this terrible economic crisis. African Americans demanded their civil rights and an end to **segregation**. Maryland experienced both good times and hard times during this century.

Harriet Tubman and the Underground Railroad

Have you heard of the Underground Railroad? It might sound like a train, but it was actually a series of safe houses for escaped slaves. The houses were owned by free African Americans in the North and their white allies. After escaping from slavery, people hid in these places as they traveled north to freedom. Harriet Tubman was one of the railroad's most famous "conductors." Tubman was a former slave. She bravely led more than 300 people to freedom. She was born in Dorchester County, Maryland, in 1822.

Lacrosse is the official team sport of Maryland.

CHAPTER 4

Culture

Maryland offers lots of fun things to see and do. Do you like to run and throw? You should try lacrosse. It is the oldest sport in North America. Native Americans have played it for hundreds of years. Do you like listening to music? Going to museums? Watching a dance performance? You'll find all of that and more in Maryland! The state has opera, theater, dance companies, and symphonies.

Sports Fans

People who love sports will find a lot to love in Maryland. There are two professional sports teams. Maryland's baseball team is the Baltimore Orioles. The football team is the Baltimore Ravens. Maryland also has an unusual state sport: jousting! This sport originated the Middle Ages. Players ride on horseback and try to spear hanging rings using a long pole called a lance.

The Baltimore Ravens get their name from "The Raven," a poem by the famous Baltimore writer Edgar Allan Poe.

Pimlico Race Course is home to the annual Preakness Stakes.

Maryland's Many Celebrations

Do you enjoy watching horse races? The Preakness Stakes is a famous race held each year in Baltimore, drawing huge crowds. Maryland also hosts many other annual events and celebrations. You can attend the Maryland Seafood Festival in Annapolis, the Maryland State Fair in Timonium, Artscape in Baltimore, and much more.

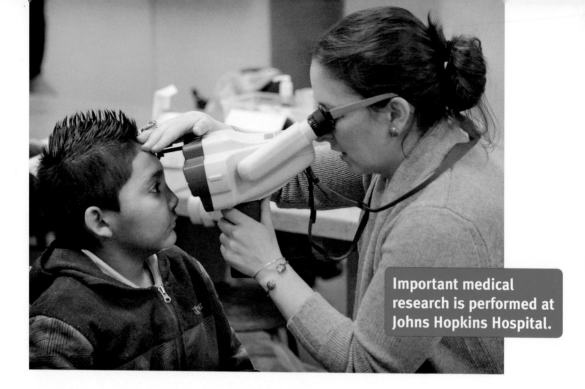

Where Do People Work?

In the past, many Maryland residents earned their living from farming, fishing, and manufacturing. Those jobs are still important, but today more people work in the service sector. Teachers, doctors, police officers, and waiters are all examples of service jobs. Many Maryland jobs are in fields related to health care and technology. One of the country's most famous hospitals, Johns Hopkins, is in Baltimore.

Education Matters

Education is important to the people of Maryland. In 1839, one of the country's first public high schools opened in Baltimore. The state has many well-known colleges and universities, including the U.S. Naval Academy in Annapolis. More than one-third of Maryland residents have a college degree. That helps them earn a good living. Although the average income in Maryland is the highest in the country, many people live in poverty.

Graduates of the U.S. Naval Academy in Annapolis throw their hats into the air in celebration.

39

Maryland's Many Flavors!

There is tasty food in every part of Maryland. Travel to the eastern side of the state and try the famous blue crabs. Trek to the valleys for fresh produce such as sweet corn, tomatoes, and apples. The city of Baltimore is home to many different **ethnic** groups. They all have favorite dishes to share. And don't leave Maryland without trying the official state dessert: the Smith Island Cake.

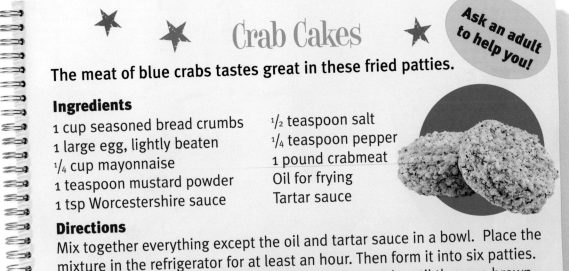

★ ★ Crab Cakes ★

Ask an adult to help you!

The meat of blue crabs tastes great in these fried patties.

Ingredients
1 cup seasoned bread crumbs
1 large egg, lightly beaten
1/4 cup mayonnaise
1 teaspoon mustard powder
1 tsp Worcestershire sauce

1/2 teaspoon salt
1/4 teaspoon pepper
1 pound crabmeat
Oil for frying
Tartar sauce

Directions
Mix together everything except the oil and tartar sauce in a bowl. Place the mixture in the refrigerator for at least an hour. Then form it into six patties. Heat the oil over medium heat. Add the patties. Cook until they are brown on one side. Flip them and do the same on the other side. Serve with tartar sauce and enjoy!

Ready to Visit Maryland?

Maryland is small, but it is full of surprises. From its coastal beaches to the forested slopes of its mountains, there are many different places to explore. Its population is diverse and multicultural, and its numerous historic sites tell many stories about America's past. You can go crabbing, watch jousting, or hike the state's many trails. Marylanders and visitors alike agree: Maryland has a little something for everyone! ★

Inner Harbour in Baltimore hosts New Year's Eve celebrations.

Famous People

Margaret Brent

(1601–1671) was a colonist in Maryland and the first woman in the New World to ask for the right to vote.

Benjamin Banneker

(1731–1806) was a free black man who lived in Maryland during the time of slavery and taught himself astronomy and mathematics. He helped survey the land that became the nation's capital.

Frederick Douglass

(1818?–1895) grew up a slave in Maryland. In 1838, he escaped and spoke out against slavery and fought for equality.

Matthew Henson

(1866–1955) was born in Maryland and became an Arctic explorer. Many people believe he was the first person to reach the North Pole.

Babe Ruth

(1895–1948) grew up in Baltimore before becoming a record-breaking baseball player. He hit 714 home runs. This record stood for 34 years.

Munro Leaf

(1905–1976) was born in Maryland. He wrote and illustrated nearly 40 children's books. His most famous character was Ferdinand, a bull who liked to smell flowers.

Rachel Carson

(1907–1964) was a conservationist and marine biologist who wrote the book *Silent Spring*. It highlighted the importance of protecting the environment. She lived and worked in Maryland.

Thurgood Marshall

(1908–1993) was a civil rights hero and the first African American Supreme Court justice. His most famous case was *Brown v. Board of Education*. It said state laws that created separate schools for black and white students were unconstitutional. He grew up in Maryland.

Vivien Thomas

(1910–1985) helped develop surgical procedures to save the lives of babies with heart defects. He also performed many operations and trained surgeons at Johns Hopkins University in Baltimore.

Michael Phelps

(1985–) was born in Baltimore. He is a famous swimmer who won 28 Olympic medals, more than any athlete in history.

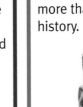

Did You Know That ...

Maryland resident Francis Scott Key wrote "The Star-Spangled Banner" after watching a battle during the War of 1812. This poem became the national anthem in 1931.

Maryland from *Terra Mariae*, or "Maria's land," was named for Queen Henrietta Maria, the wife of England's King Charles I.

Maryland was one of two states that gave land to help build the U.S. capital of Washington, D.C. The other state was Virginia.

Maryland has three nicknames: America in Miniature, because of the variety of people and geography in the state; the Old Line State, because Maryland soldiers, nicknamed the Old Line, won fame for their bravery during the Revolutionary War; and the Free State because it has long honored political and religious freedom.

Maryland's highest point is Hoye-Crest, at 3,360 feet (1,024 meters) above sea level on Backbone Mountain.

Did you find the truth?

 Maryland fought on the side of the South in the Civil War.

 The Maryland colony was founded in 1632.

Resources

Books

Nonfiction

Blashfield, Jean F. *Maryland*. New York: Children's Press, 2014.

Gigliotti, Jim. *Who Was Edgar Allan Poe?* New York: Grosset & Dunlap, 2015.

Fiction

Carbone, Elisa. *Stealing Freedom*. New York: Knopf, 1998.

Cummings, Priscilla. *A Face First*. New York: Dutton Children's Books, 2001.

Paterson, Katherine. *Jacob Have I Loved*. New York: Crowell, 1980.

Movies

Amazing Grace (1974)

Annapolis (2006)

Explorers (1985)

The Sisterhood of the Traveling Pants (2005)

Step Up (2006)

Visit this Scholastic website for more information on Maryland:

★ www.factsfornow.scholastic.com
Enter the keyword **Maryland**

Important Words

archaeologists (ahr-kee-AH-luh-jists) people who study the distant past

colony (KAH-luh-nee) a community settled in a new land but with ties to another government

endangered (en-DAYN-jurd) in danger of becoming extinct, usually because of human activity

ethnic (ETH-nik) having to do with a group of people sharing the same national origins, language, or culture

interpret (in-TUR-prit) to figure out what something means

segregation (seg-ri-GAY-shuhn) to separate or keep people away from the main group

species (SPEE-sheez) one of the groups into which animals and plants are divided

taxes (TAKS-iz) money that people and businesses must pay in order to support a government

terrain (tuh-RAYN) an area of land

Index

Page numbers in **bold** indicate illustrations.

African Americans, **21**, 31, **32**
Algonquin people, **27**
Allegheny Mountains, 10
animals, **7**, **11**, **12**, **15**, **23**, 27
Annapolis, 17, 31
Appalachian Mountains, **8**, 10
Assateague Island, **7**, **11**

Baltimore, **7**, 31, 32, 36, 37, 38, 39, 40, **41**
Blue Ridge Mountains, 10

Catoctin Mountain Park, **13**
Calvert, Cecilius, 22, 28, 30
Camp David, **7**, **13**
Charles I, 28, 30
Chesapeake Bay, **7**, **12**, 23, 28
Civil War, **30**
climate, **13**, 14
colonies, 22, 23, 25, 28, **29**, 30
constitution, 19

education, 21, **39**, 43
Eisenhower, Dwight D., 7
elections, 20, 31, 42
elevation, 45

endangered animals, 15
ethnic groups, 21, 32, 40
exploration, **28**, **42**

famous people, **42–43**
farming, 26, 30
foods, **15**, **23**, 26, 37, **40**

Great Baltimore Fire, 31
Great Britain, 28, 29, 30
Great Depression, 31

health care, **38**, 43
horses, **7**, **11**, 36, **37**

jobs, 31, **38**
Johns Hopkins hospital, 38

lacrosse, **34–35**
languages, 21

maps, **6–7**, **10**, **26**, **28**
mountains, 10, **13**, 45

national government, 7, **13**, **19**, 20, **30**, 43, **44**

Native Americans, 21, **24–25**, **26**, **27**, 28, 32, 35
nicknames, 9, 45

plants, 12, **14**, **23**, 27
population, 20, **32**
Preakness Stakes, 37

recipe, **40**
Revolutionary War, **29**, 45

settlers, **24–25**, 28
slavery, 30, 31, 33, 42
sports, **23**, **31**, **34–35**, **36**, **37**, 43
state government, **16–17**, 18
statehood, **29**, 30
symbols, 15, **22–23**

terrain, 10
timeline, **30–31**
trees, **14**, 27
Tubman, Harriet, **33**

Washington, D.C., **30**, 32, **44**
writing, **36**, 43, 44

About the Author

Vicky Franchino enjoys learning about and writing about history. She lives in Madison, Wisconsin, with her husband and their daughters.